SRA

Open Court Reading

Chinlow of Singboat

SRA

A Division of The McGraw-Hill Companies

Columbus, Ohio

www.sra4kids.com

SRA/McGraw-Hill

*A Division of The **McGraw·Hill** Companies*

Send all inquiries to:
SRA/McGraw-Hill
8787 Orion Place
Columbus, OH 43240-4027

ISBN 0-07-569971-0
    3 4 5 6 7 8 9 DBH 05 04 03 02

In the little village of Singboat lived a girl named Chinlow. She loved nature. Nature loved her.

The birds of the forest sang more sweetly for her. The doe of the forest ate from her hand. The snow on the hills shone whitest for her.

The roses Chinlow planted would always
grow tall.

"Where does Chinlow's talent come from?"
people of the village asked. "Even the rainbow
is more dazzling over Chinlow's home."

4

News of Chinlow's talent reached the emperor in faraway Pancoat.

"Could the talent of a simple child overthrow the emperor?" he wondered. "I must not let this go on."

The emperor called for his wisest teachers.
"I must know," he said, "the talent of Chinlow."
One by one the teachers spoke to Chinlow.
"Show me," each teacher said.

Chinlow looked into the face of a tiny rose. The rose Chinlow looked at began to grow until it became the loveliest rose in the garden.

Each teacher said, "I saw her talent, but I do not know it."

Finally, the emperor called Chinlow to him. "Show me," he said. Chinlow looked into the face of a tiny rose. The rose grew and became lovely. Then the emperor said to Chinlow, "Now look at me."

Chinlow looked into the emperor's eyes. The emperor saw love in her eyes. "Now I know her talent," he said, "and I am not afraid of it. Her talent is love."